Trying to get Out

To Ray Davis, my
reader and friend
Richard E. McMullen
1981

Also by the Author

Chicken Beacon

Trying

to • get

O • u • t

Richard E. McMullen

Crowfoot Softcover Series
Volume 1

CROWFOOT PRESS
ANN ARBOR MI

I gratefully acknowledge the following publications in which some of these poems have appeared: *Apple*, *The Cottonwood Review*, *The Mississippi Review*, *The Periodical Lunch*, *Seed Magazine*, *Focus/Midwest* and *Orion*.

ISBN 0-936462-50-7

Manufactured in the United States of America

MG: 9 8 7 6 5 4 3 2 1

To my Mother and my Father

Trying to get Out

WHY YOU WEED OUT SUNFLOWERS

When you raise corn, you weed out
sunflowers. If you don't, you regret it.
Sunflowers get so high.
Then they begin twisting
their heads around, watching
the sun. The young corn ears
try it, too. But they don't
have the necks for it. Some morning,
you walk out, and there's
your corn, ears on the ground
or dangling from stalks. They've wrung
their own necks, attempting
the impossible. All you have is
sunflowers, watching the sun,
as though nothing had happened.

HOW THE CORN IS DOING

Uneasy in his last sickbed,
the old man makes his way
to the back door. Sick as he is,
he has to see the corn, how
it is doing. Outside, he sees it from where
he stands. But he knows he cannot walk to it.
So, he gets down on his hands
and knees, crawling, pulling himself
to where the corn stands drinking
the damp, shadowed soil. The ears
are filling out, and the stalks are green
to the roots. Shaking his head, he chuckles
at the old fool he is;
then he crawls back to the house.

PEACHES

When he gets there, they are having a fair,
a reunion
or a funeral at the farm. Some people are watching
a heavy-set woman unloading things
from the back of a panel
truck. She has quart jars, canning jars
of peaches. She places them on shelves
that stand by
the truck and says that this is a whole new
way of burial. These
are people who have chosen
to be buried in quart jars,
as peaches, put up pits and all. Four jars
already stand on the shelves.
One of them, with a kind
of sloshing, tells the woman he's a little leery
of this and thinks he'll go back to the old
way, after all. The woman slides the jar
aside, but a man from the crowd
steps out and pushes
the jar back. No, the man says, you've
decided; you can't have it both ways! It's easy
to see the personalities mixed in with the peaches.
He can almost swear that the jar
who wants to change
is his Uncle Glenn. He walks on, out to the barn.

EARL REELY

Earl Reely had dug
in that hole by his garden for two days.
I went over
to look.
It was about a man wide,
nine feet deep. A ladder was in it.
A light cord ran down the ladder.
At its base, the hole
right-angled, tunneling under
sweet corn, tomatoes and brussels sprouts.

Earl, are you all right? I called. From the tunnel,
his face appeared, shining with clay
and sweat.
Hey! you know what I
discovered? he said. How stuff grows! It's all
done by music! You turn out
the light down here, keep still,
and you can hear it. Very slow and faint.
I'm digging to the middle, under the beets,
to hear it better. I've got to know
how it goes!
Later, it rained. Earl dug.
And the garden fell on him.

EAT SOME FOOD

He doesn't feel good.
It's not quite nausea,
not a headache
or fatique—it is more
feeling uneasy.
Eat some food,
he thinks, then you will
feel better. It has always
helped before.
He eats.

Distances
within his cells,
space wavers
briefly, a few
stars die,
certain planets
wobble away,
systems slowly
shift.

He still
doesn't feel good. He eats
a little more.

WELL, DOC, HE SAYS

Well, Doc, he says, making his voice loud
and hearty, did you fix me? Yes, says the doctor,
I fixed you. They leave the truth where it is:
deep, growing, wholly inoperable.

He tries to pray God for the pain,
but can't get past: Oh, God; oh, God.
No God is big as this pain—pain
is God. How can he pray to pain?

He wakes her, soaked with pain. Come on,
let's go—let's go! But, my dear,
she says, where can we go? I don't know,
he says, let's just get out of here.

SECRET THING

She'd always known about it,
always thought he'd stop.
Finally—I've had it!
she says. Why won't you stop? Stop
what? he says. I don't
understand. What you do, she
says. Every chance you
get. That thing you do just for
yourself. He can't answer. She
waits, thinks he'll stop.

BUT I DID SEE HIM

Somebody said I couldn't have seen him
yesterday because he died
in the hospital last week.
But I did see him. He was sitting
there. On the table edge.
Not talking.
Smoking a cigarette.
He waved casually.
I said, Haven't seen you lately.
Been sick? He grimaced
a smile, shook his head,
No, meaning, *Really sick*.
And he motioned with his smoking hand,
meaning, *I don't want to talk about it*.
Or, maybe, *Stay*
back. Anyway,
he eased himself off the table
and left. I think.
Somebody came in just then.
But I did see him.

ARABELLE'S SECRET

What will Madeline do? She has just
discovered the secret her sister Arabelle
has in her room. Madeline's elderly
eyes are wide. Turned away
from what is hanging on the wall.
A young man, naked, hooked
exactly like a fish worm. The hook,
anchor size, sticks out
in front. Arabelle has knitted a large
blue bootie for the hook.
Her cat, on its hind legs,
plays with a yarn drip. Across the room
from her sister, Arabelle smiles. Her hair
is freshly braided in a pigtail.
She is powdered, painted, dressed for the ball.
And proud. Her tall young man hangs
there so erect! Madeline must think
what to do. She wonders how she can leave
without looking again. And how
in God's name did Arabelle do it?

ZOE AT THE NURSING HOME

Strength, courage, spirit—
they rise from you like tall
trees on a run down farm.
But why do you stay here? Your old
friends, they're all sixteen
again. They've gone berrying
in the summer sun. Go
catch them, Zoe—run!

BATHROBE

On those cold, lightless mornings,
I wouldn't hear him dressing
in the dark of his bedroom,
or in the bathroom, shaving
in cold water. I'd wake when his weight
creaked the steps as he eased
downstairs. A few minutes. Then,
deep down in the basement,
he'd grab the whole house by the furnace
handle and shake it awake!

He clanks back the furnace door,
hoping he banked it right
last night and there are some hot
coals left. There aren't,
this time. He crumples newspaper,
lays kindling over it,
sets small chunks of clean
coal on the kindling, pours
oil over everything. Then he tosses
in a match. After
the first rush of fire, he throws
on a shovel of coal.

Watch. Another shovel. Now,
shut the door. Good.

A roar of fire. The vents in the furnace
door show yellow light.

Then he would get everyone up.
He had a fire going.

Not that he didn't own a bathrobe.
It hung in his closet for years.

TRYING TO GET OUT

About the turtles, George
talked me into it. I can recall feeling
shy and dumb as he talked.
If we got all their shells, he said, we could make
things with them; we could wax
them up or varnish them till they shone.
I didn't want them killed,
especially, but he said, We could make
ashtrays, paperweights and beautiful
bowls—different things for gifts.
I did want that, I thought.

These are some good things about turtles:
Snapping turtles will bite
down to the bone of your finger and hold
on, even when
you cut their heads off. Turtles live
to be over a hundred, with initials
carved in their backs to prove it. Turn
them loose and they will head
straight for the nearest water, even
if they have to cross
roads and get crushed by cars.
Inside their shells their hearts
keep beating a long time
after they're dead. George
told me all that.
                              I had twelve
turtles and kept them in
a washtub in the backyard. All
day they scratched their fine
claws on the inside, trying to get out.
Every so often,

one would lose his balance and slide
sideways, his claws raking
the metal, and land on the rim of his shell.
Then he would start again,
his claws swimming for the edge, his neck
stretched, his head pointing
like an asparagus.

George did the killing.
We put them out on the grass,
and, while they walked, he poked with the end
of a rake deep into their head
holes. I watched, but only enough
to see if it was over.

Finally, all of the turtles stopped,
their legs and tails and heads
within, hiding from danger, but still
headed, I was sure, for water.
Then we left. George told
me why, but I can't remember
why, exactly. Something about letting
the shells stand awhile.

Later, my mother phoned me at
my grandmother's: *Your turtles—they're all
in the backyard, dead. What
happened?* I could only
answer I didn't know. I knew
enough to be afraid
of knowing. I never found out
who took care of them, buried
them. My father, I suppose. I didn't.

THE PIG AND THE MAN

My friend and I were out
on Stony Creek Road,
when, seeming to burst up
out of the ditch,
were the pig and the man.
Sweating,
swearing,
the man clubbed the pig
again and again.
The pig squealed
through the high weeds,
shocked,
scared,
not knowing what to do.

SOMETHING ABOUT KEYS

When Arnold purchased his first house,
why did it have to be next to ours? His wife
worked days, and he worked nights;
their mongrel and their three beings racketed
and wrecked throughout the neighborhood;
                                        the house
and the yard went downhill fast. We yelled
at the kids and the dog; we warned Arnold
and his wife about ordinances;
                              we phoned the police—
nothing helped. They were bringing the slum
to Marvin Street. One Saturday my wife,
who was outside replanting crushed impatiens
and flattened privet, called me to the door.
Will you come and see what he wants?
                                    His wife's gone,
and he's locked himself out and can't get in.
He wants to know something about keys. What do
you mean, keys, Arnold? I asked. My tone
made him turn away.
                      He mumbled that they could be
old keys. He thought, maybe, one would fit
his lock. I was pretty sure that old
keys never fit new locks;
still I went down to the basement and got my
set. I'd often wondered what
I was saving them for. They didn't fit,
but we tried them, anyway, feeling ridiculous.
                                        For, by then,
we'd figured out how to get in without them.

CICADA

At the end of that house is the dead cicada
we buried. Two feet down—
that's deep to children. One side
of the vault is the cement wall of the house;
the other sides are stones. At the center
of the stones is an empty shotgun shell,
green, much rarer than red,
its ridged paper carefully pressed
in at the end against a disk
of tinfoil. Inside the shell is the cicada.

Of all the things we had found and saved,
this was the first we could not price.
It was not worth so many
of anything we had. It was our only
four-winged frog, poisonous,
possibly, or about to shrill. We knew
someone would steal it or we would crumble it
or it would stir to life and fly
again. So, overwhelmed and being
children, we buried the treasure in the ground.

And swore, while we dug, to return as old
men with long beards to dig it
up. We saw ourselves laugh, pound ourselves
on the back, stumble around, and then,
in silence, open the green shell
to find the cicada, still whole,
perfect, but turned by the alchemy of time
and earth to a permanent thing of jewel,
crystal, precious platings—all
we thought, when we buried it, it would become.

THE MEN WITH BULLDOZERS

In the night,
the men with bulldozers
came and covered
up just
about everything
in town. They did leave
the homes. But things
like antique and second-hand stores,
wallpaper and storm
sash stores, gas stations,
dime stores and the community
restrooms, in one
night of un-
heard earthmoving,
had gone to landfill.
My good wife said,
If you were to dig
down, you would find
a lot of good
things. All
the antiques you want, for instance.
I guess there were
a lot of good
things buried.
There might even be some
people down there. Like registered
pharmacists, funeral home
directors, used
car dealers, real estate agents,
or some of those girls
I saw on the street one night — they'd
all do anything
for the gift of excavation.

CHILDREN

I suppose you shouldn't ask some things.
But the times I have! For instance,
fall after fall, when flies who've lost
everything in the Great Frost,
show up in the school. Then there are killings!
And, more terrible: catchings.
I ask the children, as they watch
a fly's slow, circular crawl:
Doesn't a fly feel pain when you pull out
both its wings? And the children
say, No, not really. Or else:
Yes, it does. And go on with their torturings.

BEGINNERS' CONCERT

Your ears panic at irrelevance
in the snares, hysterics among the reeds,
bafflement in the brass.

                                        In unison
separately the sections frighten a white-bloused
dark-skirted tune around the air.

Pages of the score flap off
stands and under chairs.

                                        Feet
tap fifty fables about
the time.

                    Music rushes in
and out like rain-stop wind-fall bird-lull.

Your hands at concert's end applaud
the beginners prancing from the stage.

GRENISE

Grenise was always after me.
Dirty face, dirty
arms, dirty fists.
Her dusty dress made from faded
curtains. Her lardsmoke, sweat and
urine smell. She'd charge me
from her unpainted house, hollering like
a hoarse and evil grandma.
I'd cover my head as her words
turned into fists.
Grenise, what did I do?
Why are you yelling? Why
are you beating me up?
                                        We were
making a secret lean-to
with old planks. Grenise
showed up, sent the others
home, and said, We'll do it.
Later, she sat beside me
in the wooden cave. It smelled like
wet dirt, sulphur
from kitchen matches, and Grenise.
Now, she said, isn't this better?
What? I said. *I said, isn't this better!*
Yes, I said, thinking about
fists. It's better.

WALKING WITH THE DOG

My astonishment:
the moon! midnight spring—
my dog notices instantly,
watches me, ears
cocked, waiting. The master
animal will now speak to
the moon. He listens. I fail him.
We go inside, simple
creatures, lacking speech.

NEIGHBOR BOY

With instructions to clean out the weeds,
the idiot neighbor boy mowed down
fifty privet shrubs
on our line. They were stubborn—he had
to tilt the mower up
and lower it down on them, down on them
slowly. He chewed all of them
off, though, right to the dirt.
He destroyed real good.

I spoke with the boy, with his knife-
lipped sis, with his crocked
dad, with his cracked mom,
her eyes on the sun, and I spoke
with my Aetna man. What's there to do
about acts of the neighbor boy
with his mower? Little, except
to regret and, maybe, to mend.
Anyway—everything lived.

NEIGHBORS

The lawn mower was shaking itself
to death. Bolts rattled
loose and fell, the motor
shrieked and speeded up.
I turned it off, but it kept
going. Get a sledgehammer!
I yelled. Then it stopped.
It looked the same, but it
was done mowing. My big-hearted neighbor
looked it over and said:
Why, hell, I can fix
that mower for you! And he couldn't.
When I tried to pay him
for his trouble, he said: No—
that's what neighbors are for.

WORKING ON THE ROOF

Climbing up
to the roof isn't bad. The roof seems high, though,
and steep. He straddles the central
ridge. From old shingles, sand
slides to the ground.
He grips with his feet,
knees, backside—anything. He feels
the job's particular pain.
He can't escape it.
The sun is much hotter.
He starts shingling. The rows he nails increase.
Now he works
with both hands. He stops thinking about what's
beneath him. He likes the sound
he makes. It's his own.
People shout things up
in one language;
he shouts down in another. He's taller
than many things around him.
Climbing off the roof is bad.
It's always bad.

WE ARE IN BACK, THE DOG IS IN FRONT

We are in back. The dog is in front.
I watch a girl go by,
holding a white chicken, feeding
it corn. When the ball rolls
into the street, the dog chases
after. My wife shouts.
I wave my arms. But a red
VW has him,
covering all but his head, like a giant
snail. I press my stocking
cap to my eyes. Getting over
the fences takes forever;
I wish I'd never put them up.
Just as I get there, the driver
runs his car on over the dog.
I see the remains: like three
furry strips of cleaned fish.
The driver turns into
our drive, rolls clear back
to our garage. Harold—
it is my old friend Harold!
He nods and smiles; he waves.

YOU WERE SWEEPING

I was watching you sweeping the rug in your pink
slacks, when you turned the sweeper off,
stood close to me shyly, and said,
Have you ever, in your mind
or your dreams, been in love with someone else?
Yes, I said, who do you love
that way? Napoleon, you said.
I would never be unfaithful,
but I had to tell someone about it.
I know, I said, it's the way
things are. Everyone has those dreams;
there's nothing we can do about it.
We looked far into each other's eyes;
then you went back to your sweeping.

THE VISITANTS

Nine black and
yellow goldfinch dart
into flowers I never weed,
to spend a few days
at the garden's heart,
feeding on a certain seed.

FLAT SURFACES

I spent years in bars and restaurants,
sitting at flat surfaces, drinking
and eating, smoking and smiling — waiting
for what was supposed to happen. When I'd
walk in, someone would say, We're all
here; now it can start. At closing,
I'd rise to leave, and someone would say,
Well, it didn't happen; let's go.
I felt like an extra in a movie,
hired for a scene that was never played.
The hell with it! — who needed a job
like that? So I quit. But I'm still waiting
for what's supposed to happen, still
sitting at other flat surfaces.

HOLES

At the edge of the Acid Hop,
I watch the students listen
to the rock from the stage. The rock
and the drugs have made good holes in them.
They are held together
by holes. Alone in public,
they listen privately. Strangers
from outside join strangers
inside. I watch with half
sight, unable to see
or hear more than part, not
wanting their wholeness but hating
to be left out. I
am solid; I have no rock,
no acid holes. I have
no holes within holes. Nothing
goes through me. Everything bounces
away or swings around me.
And, all the time, this old
child, no taller
than my waist, his hair to the shoulders,
his face flushed, his brain
sloshing and leaking through millions
of holes, his body solid
holes, circles me like a panther.
What are you? he keeps
asking. A Jesus Christer?
What are you, anyway?

HAVING IT

I am striding along Miller Avenue toward the school
with Big Bill Malcolm. At Forsythe Junior High
teachers hope Bill will speak to them (respectfully).
Seventh Grade boys hope Bill will lift them up
by the head (carefully) or do something else friendly.
Girls just hope—what, they don't really
know. Bill is an all-round student, except
academically. When he is around,
everyone feels uneasy
because Bill has it, whatever having
it is. Bill, I say, you are at least two
feet taller than I am. Oh, no, you
taller than me, Teach, Big Bill says.

WILLIE MILLARD

Willie Millard was thirteen. He looked thirty.
He didn't take any one drug—
he took everything. Once he sniffed
solvent from a paper bag.
All day, he told people one joke,
cracking up each time.

Once Willie shuffled up and asked for lunch money.
How much do you need, Willie? I said,
thinking maybe thirty-five cents.
Five bucks, he said.

Once, hiding out in my class,
he tried explaining things: If I
hadn't been born, he said, then there wouldn't be
this room with me in it,
and the principal wouldn't be around,
trying to bust me and get me in trouble.

One icy morning, an awful thing happened.
Willie was walking to school
down the middle of the street.
He was dazed and messed up, as always.
A fast-moving car came up behind him.
The driver hit the horn, braked, skidded.
Willie didn't even look around.
And the car missed him.

ROOSTER

He had no business at all doing
what he did: getting
up out of bed early, going
downstairs and putting
on that foolish rooster's head
from the party. There he sat
at the kitchen table when his wife walked in,
poor dear. He went: Er er Er er
ER, trying to sound like a rooster
at dawn but coming out
more like a wicked, mocking child.
She, still half
asleep, sought explanations,
chose a wrong one and fainted
on the spot. He hopped over
to where she lay, shook her
with his claw, then, when she didn't
flutter, lost all
interest. The house was, all at once,
too small. He needed
room to scratch, to flap his wings,
a high place to work on his crowing.

HOLIDAY WEEKEND

January first he looked out the window
just as the sun went by.

Look! he said.
A robin redbreast!

That's no
robin, she said. That's the sun.

I mean in the tree there.

That's an apple.

You're right. A bad one. Impaled
on the tree. A seed fallen on no
ground at all. Pathetic.

What, she said,
your sight? Your hangover?

No. Everything
else.

ROAST BEEF

When he started his sermons,
we looked at Rev. Leaf—
crew cut, medium rare face,
juicy body—and our stomachs
gurgled. We choked on saliva. Bent in pain.
Lost side vision. We heard
stomachs around us, stomachs in rows, stomachs in
congregation. Rev. Leaf heard, too, paused, and
sat down. We sang a last intestinal hymn.
When he preached,
we thought about roast beef, mashed
potatoes and gravy, cheeses and apple pie.
We made him leave. He made us hungry.

THE CHANGE

I've got the change, he told the clerk.
He groped in the crumbs, junk
and lint for some coins.
And found the hand. It was cold,
wet, lost. It vised
his hand, yanked it
hard. He just got free. My God,
he said. I can't help you.
I don't have the change, he said.

LEONARD LUTZ

Slams his tools down on the
bench. Ten o'clock in the
morning. He's into his coat and
hat. Where the hell are
you going, Leonard? someone
yells. I been married
to my wife for twenty
years, he says, and I never
seen her naked. I'm
going home, by God!